A few concise examples of seven hundred errors in Shakespeare's plays, now corrected and elucidated, etc.

Zachariah Jackson, William Shakespeare

A

FEW CONCISE EXAMPLES

OF

SEVEN HUNDRED ERRORS

IN

Shakspeare's Plays,

Now Corrected and Elucidated;

AND WHICH HAVE AFFORDED ABUNDANT SCOPE FOR CRITICAL ANIMADVER-
SION; AND HITHERTO HELD AT DEFIANCE THE PENETRATION OF
ALL SHAKSPEARE'S COMMENTATORS.

BY ZACHARIAH JACKSON.

London:

PRINTED FOR THE AUTHOR,
By *John Hill, No. 32, Water Lane, Blackfriars;*
AND SOLD BY
JAMES HARPER, BOOKSELLER, 46, FLEET STREET.

1818.
(PRICE SIXPENCE.)

ADDRESS.

WE have had some, but not many, instances where the fostering hand of patronage has been denied to genius: this, my predecessors never experienced; they found no difficulty in obtaining a liberal compensation for their labours from the Booksellers; for, celebrity of name stamped merit on whatever their genius produced, and was considered "a tower of strength" by their respective publishers. But whether my production possesses merit or not; whether it displays superiority, or is inferior to their *comments*, it has been alike rejected by every bookseller to whom I offered it for publication. But I cannot blame those gentlemen; prejudice has operated with equal force on their minds as on the learned critics', and wherefore, but from the angry lash which illiberal criticism has laid on my predecessors.

Of all the Critics, perhaps none has displayed such unjust censures as the author of the PURSUITS OF LITERATURE; who, declaiming against Shakspeare's Commentators, in general, reprobates several thousand notes, and advances FIVE INSIGNIFICANT EXAMPLES as a criterion for the WHOLE; and by which, in his *anxious Pursuits* he strives to make the literary world converts to his own illiberal opinion: — These five Examples are, first, Observations on a *Gib-cat:* — second, On the *Old Vice:* — third, On the *stimulating power of potatoes:* — fourth, On *Stewed Prunes:* and fifth, On *Coney-catching!* From these examples, he says, the entire labour of all Shakspeare's Commentators may be judged. Whether then must such observations be attributed to illiberality, or deficiency of judgment? That he has prejudiced the public against Shakspeare's Commentators is but too true; and, that he has deterred the Booksellers from giving encouragement to such productions, however sanctioned by private approbation, I have strongly experienced, and which thus compels me to solicit the patronage of Shakspeare's admirers, that the honour of the Immortal Bard may, in a greater degree, be redeemed from those unjust censures which have found a passage even into foreign countries.

THE AUTHOR.

London, Sept. 14, 1818.

A

FEW CONCISE EXAMPLES

OF

SEVEN HUNDRED ERRORS

IN

Shakspeare's Plays,

Now Corrected and Elucidated.

The Edition of Shakspeare, commonly denominated Johnson and Steevens' Shakspeare, 21 vols. 8vo. is that to which the pages refer; but as the Acts and Scenes of the Play are also specified, the reader can find the passage with facility in any other edition.

" Eternal verdure bloom in Shakspeare's grove!
" Where led by light from heav'n, he oft would rove
" In solitude and sacred silence blest;
" And in the musings of his mighty breast,
" All as he scann'd the volume of the past,
" O'er Greece and Rome one wistful glance would cast;
" Mourn not, pleas'd nature cried, their sounds unknown,
" My universal language is your own."

PURSUITS OF LITERATURE.

THE ingenious Author of the above verses, in his satirical animadversions on Shakspeare's Commentators, whom he terms, Black Letter Dogs, opposing them with tiger-like ferocity to tear the vitals of Literature from their bosoms, marks his own extraordinary penetration thus :

" Enough for me great Shakspeare's words to hear,
" Though but in common with the vulgar ear ;
" *Without one note,* or horn-book in my hand, &c.

From this display of confidence, the learned critic would impress on our understanding, that the edition of Shakspeare, as published by Hemminge and Condell, in 1623, is so perfectly clear and divested of obscurity, that (even to the *vulgar mind,*) correction, restoration, and elucidation are unnecessary. If then an illiterate person can thus easily pierce through corruption, and penetrate Shakspeare's meaning in those passages, which, like rich gems enveloped in their crust, are totally obscured ; I should be glad to know what construction the

B

learned critic, or any literary character, would put on the following corrupt passage in

ROMEO AND JULIET.

ACT. III. SCENE 2. *page* 144.

JULIET.   Spread thy close curtain love performing night!
           That *run-aways* eyes may wink.

On the compound word, *run-aways*, an infinity of learned comment has been expended, but all in vain : yet, according to the orthography of Shakspeare's time, the transposition of a single letter gives the original word; and produces so clear a meaning, that neither the Greek of Judge Blackstone, nor the laboured elucidations of the other Commentators are necessary. Our great Poet wrote :

> Spread thy close curtain, love performing night!
> That *unawares*, eyes may wink: and Romeo
> Leap to these arms untalk'd of, and unseen !

Juliet invokes night to mantle the world in darkness, that, by a heavy atmosphere, sleep may steal *unawares* upon the eye-lids of those who would obstruct her pleasures ; and, that then, *Romeo may leap to her arms, untalked of, and unseen.*

What can possibly be more simple ? Now see how the error originated.—The old mode of spelling *unawares*, was *unawayrs :*—the word had what Printers term, a literal error ; that is, such as an *o* for an *r ;* in the correcting of which having taken out the *o*, he placed the *r* at the beginning of the word, and thus turned *unawayrs* to *runaways*.

In speaking of the *Old-Vice*, a character introduced in our ancient Comedies, the author of the *Pursuits of Literature* has been rather moderate ; indeed, he seems to have introduced Mr. Upton's definition of the *Old-Vice*, merely for the purpose of reprobating those acts of horror which that hydra-headed monster, Revolution, had occasioned in France.   But, it is to be lamented, that the critic's extraordinary penetration did not solve what has proved an enigma too difficult for the learned: I mean the *formal Vice*, to whom Gloster is made to compare himself, in

KING RICHARD III.

ACT III. SCENE 1. *page* 371.

GLOSTER.   Thus like the *formal Vice*, iniquity,
            I moralize two meanings in one word.

The adjective *formal*, according to its general acceptation, is totally unconnected with *Vice*.   Mr. Upton says, " *Vice* seems to be an abbreviation of Vice-*devil*: as Vice-*roy*, Vice-*doge*:" from which we must infer, that the *Old Vice* was the Devil's deputy: yet, behold how Commentators differ. Mr. Douce, who has been indefatigable in his researches, in speaking of the *Vice*, says, " He was a bitter enemy to the devil, and a part of his employment consisted in teasing and tormenting the poor fiend on all occasions." If the reader takes the trouble to examine Johnson and Steevens' edition of Shakspeare, 1813, he will find nearly ten pages of small print introduced to illustrate the *formal Vice*: a character which the indefatigable researches of the Commentators has never been able to ascertain; nor even, that a plurality of *Vices* were ever characterized in scenic representation. But let me hasten to display the error, and thereby confirm the literati, that a *Vice*, called the *formal Vice*, was never introduced in the Old Moralities; nor, as I may venture to say, ever met with in any author, save in the corrupt passage wherein we now behold it.

More than once we hear Richard descanting on the imperfect state of his body: he well knows his appearance to be hideous, and he seems to glory that his mind corresponds with it. Thus, alike vicious in mind and body, he views the external; and feeling the internal workings of a guilty, hypocritical mind, he, in few, but expressive words, paints himself a devil.

> Thus like the *form*, *all* vice, iniquity
> I moralize ;—two meanings in one word.

Thus Gloster, though he moralizes on his own hypocrisy and falsehood, speaks so clearly the language of truth, that elucidation is unnecessary.

The word *formal*, according to the old mode of spelling, was *formall*: surely then any person can perceive how the error originated: the compositor having omitted to put a space between *form* and *all*, joined the two words; by which the sequent word, *Vice*, became a person, and *formal* its adjective.

But what proves the error beyond controversy is, that *iniquity* is made the *formal Vice*: see the reading—" Thus like the *formal Vice*, iniquity." So that Gloster moralizes like *iniquity*; instead of which, it is his own *iniquity* that he moralizes, and produces two meanings from one word.

In such cases I have no defence to offer for those highly eminent characters, who laboured with unceasing toil to bring order out of confusion, and to elucidate the great Poet of Nature: but infallibility belongeth not to man; for, though the star of genius often beamed on many of Shakspeare's Commentators, yet, as I shall prove, in SEVEN HUNDRED instances, the cloud of obscurity enveloped its rays, and veiled from their view several of the most striking beauties inventive genius could produce, or nature's most luxuriant valley yield, for poetic scenery. To bring those beauties to perfect light; to defend the author's

text, where unjustifiable alterations have been made; and to re-
move all corruption from it, was *a solace to my afflictions during the latter part of Eleven Years captivity in France.*

But prejudice is armed against me, in common with all
Shakspeare's Commentators. The public have an edition of
his works in 21 volumes, of which, exclusive of the Prologema,
nearly one half may be considered as Notes; and indeed, many
hundred of them are unnecessary; nor can I see but one justi-
fiable reason why the editor, if he had discrimination, did not
select the most judicious and omit the rest: which reason I pre-
sume to be, that, as the Commentators in general, were aware
that they had not recovered the true reading; and, in other
cases, where the text had a sort of enigmatical form, which their
penetration had not clearly developed, he submitted the
respective opinions to the reader's judgment. But what critic, however versed with our Poet's style, could decide while
corruption still remained; as will be seen in the SEVEN HUN-
DRED passages, wherein I have either recovered, or restored the
original, and elucidated, as I trust, according to the spirit of
the author.

That the Commentators had no confidence in their various
opinions, they have, in many instances, given us decided proofs;
for we find after a long discussion, their conclusive arguments
terminated by—*All attempts at restoration seems vain:* or, *this
passage is irremidiably corrupt:* or, *I do not approve even of
my own emendation.* Admitting then, an average of four opinions on each of those SEVEN HUNDRED errors that I profess
to correct and illustrate; my notes, if sanctioned by the literary
world, must reduce nearly *three thousand* notes; for controversy on false principles, however ably supported, must yield to
characteristic uniformity and context, where demonstration is often produced, even from the very letters, where corruption
is conspicuous; and in many instances, where the variation is
not more than a single letter; as in the following examples:

KING LEAR.

Act II. Scene 2. *page 395.*

Kent.   *Three-suited knave,*

Surely it requires no degree of argument to convince, even the
most fastidious critic, that our author wrote — *Tree*-suited
knave: *meaning,* a rogue *suited* for, or who deserves Tyburn
tree.

Act IV. Scene 3. *page 526.*

Kent.   A sovereign shame *so elbows* him.

How my predecessors could, in any manner, reconcile this
absurd reading is truly extraordinary! *So elbows him!* who

ludicrous! But see what the change of a single letter effects; and what sublimity is introduced in the place of meanness, if not of nonsense. Our author wrote:

A sovereign shame *soul bows* him : his own unkindness
That stripp'd her from his benediction, turn'd her
To foreign casualties, gave her dear rights
To his dog-hearted daughters—these things sting
His mind so venemously, that burning shame
Detains him from Cordelia.

A sovereign shame so oppresses the soul of Lear for his unnatural treatment of the virtuous Cordelia, that he cannot command sufficient resolution to behold her.

Any reader who thinks this phrase requires an example will find one almost *verbatim* in Psalm 57.

This error owes its origin to the person who read to the transcriber; he sounded the word *soul*, (*so-el*), which coming before *bows*, the transcriber gave the present corrupt reading.

HAMLET.

ACT I. SCENE 2. *page* 42.

HAMLET.   I am glad to see you : good even, Sir.

This passage has been totally misunderstood; and that it should, I am not at all surprised; for the punctuation would deceive the most minute critic. The word *even*, according to the acceptation it must receive in it present position, means, *to make one party out of debt with another, either in point of pecuniary obligation or compliment:* in the latter sense, Hamlet's familiar politeness induces him to use it: but false punctuation has perverted the sense of the passage, and made my predecessors, under the persuasion that it alluded to *the time of the day,* attempt its illustration. See the punctuation corrected.

MARCELLUS.   My *good* lord,
HAMLET.   I am glad to see you *good :* — *even,* Sir.

Hamlet plays on the word *good;* and though it is understood to mean — *well;* he, at the same time, tells Marcellus, that he is *even with him* in courtesy of expression.

SECOND PART OF KING HENRY IV,

ACT II. SCENE 2. *page* 57.

POINS.   The answer is as ready as a *borrower's cap:*

The turn which Dr. Warburton's injudicious correction has given this passage, while it produces a meaning, creates an additional error, and places the sense of the author at a greater distance from critical penetration. The old copy reads:

" The answer is as ready as a *borrowed cap:*"

But that which has been *borrowed* must be again restored : as also, what the stupid transcriber robbed our poet of more than two centuries ago — a *borrowed cant.*

What is that *borrowed cant?*

"I am the King's poor cousin, Sir."

A cant phrase reflecting on the poverty of those who claimed consanguinity with the king, but whose wants remained unrelieved. This cant phrase, we are to suppose, was *borrowed* on many occasions.

In Shakspeare's Age, the *n* and *u* being in general formed alike, the compositors were often led into errors ; as in the following ludicrous blunder :

MUCH ADO ABOUT NOTHING.

Act V. Scene 1. *page* 144.

LEONATE.   Make misfortune drunk
        With *candle-wasters.*

The antecedent part of this speech displays the feelings of a fond parent, labouring under the afflicting wound his honour has received, in the base defamation of his guiltless child : so great indeed his affliction, that it refuses every consoling balm which friendship offers. To ordinary calamities, no doubt he would have been submissive ; but the oppressive weight of his grief, he conceives beyond human power to bear, and that no person could measure woe with his woe, and " *hem when he should groan,*" or " *patch grief with proverbs ;*" which being, as he conceives, incompatible with real affliction, he starts a third impossibility ; and, if any person labouring under equal distress of mind can do these things, *bring him hither,* says he, " *and I of him will gather patience.*"—That which Leonate now requires is, to " *make misfortune drunk with candle-wasters :*"—So says the text.

Had Mr. Steevens reflected, that it is impossibilities which the unhappy Leonate proposes, he would not have sent a person labouring under affliction to a tavern, there to sit during the night in dissipated company, and to get drunk by swallowing *flap-dragons !*—Surely a more effectual method to make misfortune drunk could not be suggested.

But the beverage to which Leonate alludes is, truly, of a simple nature ; sick it might make any person who would drink of it profusely, but drunk, never. Shakspeare wrote :

                Make misfortune drunk
        With *caudle-waters.*

The compositor having composed *candle* instead of *caudle,* concluded, that as there was no such thing as *candle-water,* it must be *candle-wasters ;* and thus adding an *s,* he, with the art of Dr. Faustus, turned *caudle-waters* into *candle-wasters.*

It has been asserted, by those who have made enquiry concerning the learning and genius of Shakspeare, that he was unlettered; that is, his Latin was little, and his Greek less. Without these, however, he contrived to shine with splendour; and, like Goldsmith's Professer, (without Greek) what he sought, he obtained. But with the modern languages, such as French and German, particularly the former, I believe Shakspeare to have been rather conversant; and of this I would give a strong proof, but that the illustration of the passage would take up more space than I can afford in these few pages. However, to show that his Commentators should have paused before they so positively asserted his deficiency—I shall give a proof of their own fallibility.

ALL'S WELL THAT ENDS WELL.

Act II. Scene 1. *page* 278.

Lafeu. Why your Dolphin is not *lustier.*

Lustier is certainly English, and sufficiently expressive to afford a sort of meaning; but the Commentators have left it a matter undecided, whether Lafeu means the *Dauphin,* (a title given to the eldest son of the French King;) or *Dolphin,* (a fish.) But while arguments, in support of opinion on one side, and answers to confute on the other, were encreasing notes, the corrupt word remained unnoticed.

When the king, after being cured, enters with Helena, Parolles says to Lafeu, "Here comes the King."—To which Lafeu adds, "*Lustick,* as the Dutchman says."—Now, the German word, *lustig,* and the Teutonic, *lustick,* are the same, and mean *playful* or *sportive;* the comparative of which adjective is—*lustiger,* meaning, *more playful:* here then is the error. Lafeu, sports his German on the occasion, and says—

Why your Dolphin is not *lustiger.*

Meaning, that the king was now so perfectly recovered, he had become as sportive and playful as a Dolphin; for, of all fishes, the Dolphin is most given to sport.

To compare the king in stature or corpulency to a small fish is ridiculous; and we know not whether his son be either lusty or playful.

In Antony and Cleopatra, Act V. Scene 2. The sportive manner of Antony is thus compared to a Dolphin.

"———————————————— His delights
" Were dolphin-like; they shew'd his back above
" The element they liv'd in."

Thus the addition of a *g,* settles this strongly controverted point. The manner in which the error took place is obvious.—The Compositor, or, perhaps, the transcriber, being unacquainted with the German word, *lustiger,* concluded it must be *lustier;* and therefore, omitted the *g,* not doubting himself perfectly correct.

It is not altogether by recovering the original words that notes may be reduced; but also, by displaying to the minute investigator the erroneous elucidations of my learned predecessors; as in the following puzzle, which confounded their penetration.

TAMING OF THE SHREW.

Act. III. Scene 2. *page* 105.

BIONDELLA. Why Petruchio is coming, in a new hat, and an old jerkin; a pair of old breeches, thrice turned; a pair of boots that have been candle-cases, one buckled, another laced; an old rusty sword ta'en out of the town armory, with a broken hilt, and chapeless, with *two broken points.*

Two broken points! All the commentators concur in opinion, that this passage is corrupt: "For how a sword could have two broken points," says Dr. Johnson, "I know not." Mr. Steevens thinks there was a deficiency in the broad and rich belt of Petruchio, and that the *broken points* refer to it. But notwithstanding the various opinions on this two-pointed puzzle, nothing is clearer than that the sword which Petruchio took out of the town armory had *two broken points;* and, that the character may, in future, be furnished with a sword to correspond with the author's words, I shall explain this extraordinary paradox!— Petruchio's sword, notwithstanding all its other deficiencies, had—a scabbard; but unfortunately, that scabbard had a *broken point; i. e.* had lost its *tip,* nay, perhaps wanted one-fourth of its due length; thus his *broken-pointed* sword, (*the blade;* for the blade is but a part of the sword,) had a full opportunity of peeping out; and, to the amazement of Biondella, discovered that this famous sword had—*two broken points!*

Had the blade been shorter than the scabbard; notwithstanding the scabbard had lost its *tip,* or point, one broken point only, could be seen.

In repeated instances I have found the author's sense perverted by false transcription, arising from the hissing sound of *s's,* particularly where the terminating *s* of one word, has been carried in sound to the next; as in

ANTONY AND CLEOPATRA.

Act IV. Scene 13. *page* 252.

CLEOPATRA: Here's *sport* indeed:—How heavy weighs my lord!

To force an appropriate meaning from this passage, in its present state, is beyond every effort of human genius; and the solemnity of the occasion on which the word *sport* has been used, proves, that Shakspeare's immortal genius has been sported with too long.—Be it observed, that CLEOPATRA is in the *Monument*, attended by CHARMIAN and IRIS; and Antony, at the point of death, is borne in by his guards.

The gross blunder that strips this passage of a beauty replete with genius, must be attributed to the transcriber, who from the hissing sound of the *s's*, lost two letters of a word, and carried the terminating one to the sequent word. Our great Bard wrote :

Here's *his port*, indeed :—How heavy weighs my lord !

The *monument* becomes the port ; there ANTONY, (the vessel,) is tugged or drawn in, by CLEOPATRA and her attendants, (the mariners ;) and there, the great vessel that had borne many a tempestuous gale, becomes a final wreck.

MERCHANT OF VENICE.
ACT III. SCENE 2. *page* 318.

BASSANIO.   But her eyes,—
How could he see to do them ? having made one,
Methinks it should have power to steal both his,
And leave *itself* unfinish'd.

In painting, the artist must finish one eye before he can give corresponding beauty to the other. This is the figure which strikes Bassanio : he wonders when the painter had made one eye, that its beauty did not steal both his, —

And leave *it's self* unfinish'd.

i. e. *Its fellow eye.* By the word *unfinished,* he means the ornaments of the eye : the eye-brows, &c.

In this blunder there is some apology for the transcriber : for no ear can distinguish *itself* from *its self*, unless a short pause be observed between *its* and *self*.

The delicate idea which this passage now conveys, is, I believe, original : I do not recollect meeting, in our Author's Works, its similitude.

In the present improved state of printing few errors are attributable to the proprietors of printing offices ; but, in Shakspeare's time, from the ignorance of compositors, and the carelessness of pressmen, every work abounded with them. But it must be admitted, that a manuscript, if carelessly written ; that is, if replete with blots and interlineations, which is often the case, it could not be done justice to, even at the present day, unless the author inspects the proofs ; for words are frequently mistaken by the compositor, and often he is obliged, by making out a letter or two in each word of a sentence, to form a chain, perhaps of totally different links to those with which they must be connected. With such blunders Shakspeare's plays abound : I shall exhibit a few examples :

MACBETH.

Act III. Scene 1. *page* 157.

MACBETH.   Within this hour at most,
  I will advise you where to plant yourselves.
  Acquaint you with *the perfect spy o'the time,*
  The moment on't;

On the various and unqualified explications given of this extraordinary passage, I shall be silent; merely observing, that in
its present corrupt state, all elucidation has been thrown away.

Before I correct the passage, it is necessary that I make a
few observations. Macbeth tells the murderers to *meet him
within an hour, when he will tell them where to plant themselves.* Now, are we to suppose that these murderers were acquainted with the various avenues, entrances, windings, &c. of
the park? Could they know at which gate Bancho would enter?
Certainly not: nor are we to suppose that this was more than
the second time they had been within the court of Inverness.
Of all this Macbeth is well aware, and therefore he provides
accordingly.

Now, as the murder is to be perpetrated near the inner court
of the palace, it becomes necessary, for two reasons, that the
murderers should be made acquainted with the different avenues
leading towards it: first, that when Macbeth advises them
where to plant themselves, they may know the *particular place*
from his description of it; for, it is not to be supposed that
Macbeth would be so incautious as to be seen walking about his
park with these suspicious looking characters; for, should they
be taken in the sanguinary deed, the instigator of it would be
conspicuous: and secondly, that when the murder is perpetrated,
the avenue to escape by, may be familiar to the murderers.
These are the present objects of Macbeth's consideration; and,
that they may make themselves acquainted with the different
avenues, entrances, &c. he gives them an hour to make the
necessary observations; during which time, he will endeavour to
learn by what road Bancho will return.

That the author's original corresponded with the above necessary considerations, I am convinced; and to obtain which, I
am equally convinced he wrote:

    Within this hour at most,
  I will advise you where to plant yourselves:
  Acquaint you with the *precincts by* the time:
  The moment on't.

i. e. Make yourselves acquainted with the *precincts* of the
castle by that time: go about it immediately.

Thus the verse maintains its due measure.

In the First part of King Henry VI. Act. II. sc. 1. the same word is used in alluding to a particular boundary.

> CHARLES. " And for myself most part of all the night,
> " Within her quarter, and mine own *precinct*,
> " I was employ'd in passing to and fro,
> " About relieving of the sentinels."

The words *precincts by* and *perfect spy* are composed of nearly the same letters, and have the same number: but the word *precincts* was unknown, or not familiar to the compositor, and probably having been, at first, equally so to the transcriber, he, in correcting, blotted the words, and thus created an insurmountable difficulty to the compositor.

The following passage in the same Scene, *page* 158, being equally corrupt, I introduce it; as, when corrected, it confirms the preceding illustration.

> MACBETH. And something from the palace; *always thought*,
> That I require a clearness.

The meaning which this passage demands is,—Let it be some distance from the palace; and at a place from whence you may easily effect your escape; for should you be taken, having been seen here, suspicion will fall on me, that I hired you to slay them: therefore, I require a clearness.

Can the most fastidious critic doubt the following being the Author's text:

> And something from the palace; *a way though*,
> That I require a clearness.

Three superfluous letters have been introduced to render this passage corrupt: an *l*, an *s*, and a *t*. Which in the copy were nothing more than false flourishes, (a practice common with many writers at the termination of each word,) but taken by the compositor for letters. Any person who thinks proper to try the experiment by turning the terminating part of the *a* round and rather elevated, will find it to resemble an *l:* the *y* in *alway*, by giving a curl round, which is common, will have the appearance of an *s;* and the *h*, by bringing the round stroke quick, and a second down-stroke has the appearance of an imperfectly formed *t.*—To one who has had a variety of manuscripts through his hands, the manner in which such errors took place is obvious.

ACT IV. SCENE 1. *page* 201.

2nd WITCH. Thrice; and once the hedge-pig whin'd.

Both Mr. Theobald and Mr. Steevens mistook the force of this passage:—When the second Witch spoke, the *hedge-pig* had *whin'd* but once: See the subsequent note.

PAGE 202.

3rd WITCH.   *Harper* cries; 'Tis time, 'tis time.

In this scene we perceive a cauldron, in which must be supposed various ingredients for composing an infernal broth. In
the progress of this magical preparation the witches await certain signals: *the mewing of the brindled cat* three times, is the
first. The *hedge-pig* has *whin'd* once; but before the witches
can proceed in their infernal ceremony, the *hedge-pig* must
repeat its cries, to make the magical number *thrice*, and
which they await. Scarcely hath the second witch finished her
observation, that the *hedge-pig had whin'd once*, when that
animal *whines* again and again; which announces the critical
moment for the witches to proceed in their infernal ceremony,
and immediately the third witch exclaims:

Hark, her cries! 'Tis time, 'tis time.

Then they go round about the cauldron and throw in the
additional ingredients.

It is almost unnecessary to say, that the transcriber, who
wrote as another person read to him, mistook the sound of the
words, and, for — *Hark her*, wrote — *Harper*. '

Some Commentator supposes *Mr. Harper* to have been a
familiar spirit ; but, in my opinion, *Mr. Harper* was as little
known to Shakspeare as to any of his Commentators.

And here it may not be intrusive to observe, why I speak
with such confidence. I admit that in point of erudition and
extensive reading, most of my predecessors, were my superiors;
but nature, perhaps, has not been less bountiful in granting me
both penetration, and a discriminating judgment: add to these
I have more than an equivalent for their extensive erudition
and minute acquaintance with the ancient classics, I am inti-
mately acquainted with the printing business in all its branches;
have had a *practical knowledge* of it, at least, thirty years; have
been the proprietor of an extensive Printing Office; have had
manuscripts of every description through my hands ; know how
the compositors make these blunders; and, having read for the
press, have scrutinized every species of careless writing : Thus
I venture to assert, *that I have a material advantage over all
my predecessors in developing the errors, and in correcting
them ;* and, I trust that my elucidations will make our immortal poet be satisfactorily understood.

A vast number of errors have gained footing in Shakspeare's
works through the carelessness of transcribers. It has been
sufficiently authenticated by my predecessors, that transcripts
were, in general, made from the detached parts given by the
players to the publisher; which parts were read to the transcriber, and the copy thus produced, sent immediately to the

printer. That our author became, by this means, doubly exposed to blunders, exclusive of those incident in a printing office, we need not be surprised; for the person who read, if he had a bad articulation, and the transcriber an unchaste ear, words most familiar to the comprehension of the latter, would, unquestionably, be inserted; and that this has been the case, my predecessors have proved in various instances; though, *of this description*, they have left more than two hundred for me to develop, of which I give the following as examples.

THE TEMPEST.

Act I. Scene 2. *page 25.*

PROSPERO.   Now *I arise:*
Sit still and hear the last of our sea-sorrow.

Sir William Blackstone demands, "Why does Prospero arise?" He then proposes to give the words—"Now I arise," to Miranda. But why should Miranda arise; she who has manifested so lively an interest in the narrative of her father? however, it is very evident, from the sequent verse, that she attempts to move from her seat, but is prevented by Prospero; the reason of which will be obvious when the author's words are recovered. I read:

Now *ire, rise!*
Sit still and hear the last of our sea-sorrow.

Prospero, in the course of his narration, smothers all indignation against his brother; but now the retrospect of his treachery figures to his imagination all the dangers and all the calamities he has endured; and which *raising* the passion of vengeance in his bosom, he exclaims — Now *ire, rise!* which words, from his enraged look, attitude, and action, awaking sensations of fear in the breast of Miranda, she attempts to move from her seat; but judging the true cause of her emotion, Prospero curbs his indignant fury, and modulating his voice, tells her to "Sit still, and hear" him recount "the last of their sea-sorrows," and the care he had taken of her education.

The transcriber made the blunder: *I arise* and *ire, rise!* have, perhaps, as close a similarity of sound as any two words formed of different characters.

WINTER'S TALE.

Act I. Scene 2. *page 240.*

LEONTES.   My wife's a hobby horse; deserves a name
As rank as any flax-wench that *puts to*
Before her troth-plight.

This passage, though very corrupt, is not altogether obscure ; a meaning may be obtained, but totally foreign from the figure which the author's words display.

> My wife's a hobby-horse ; deserves a name
> As rank as any flax-wench that *buts tow*
> Before her troth-plight.

To but tow is the business of the flax-wench, who twists the *tow* into a hank ; and this is called *butting,* because it confines all the fibres of the tow, and each end becomes a *but-end.*

In the act of butting, the flax-wench is compelled to place herself in an indelicate position : and when the first but-end is perfected, it is placed in a manner that would create risibility in a libertine, and draw a blush from female delicacy. The *troth-plight* is a sort of apron, before which she *buts the tow ;* and a *troth-plight* is also a sweetheart ; or, one to whom a female has plighted her troth : therefore, *butting tow before him,* conveys ideas that hold no affinity with chastity.—Thus our ingenious bard plays on the words, to mark the supposed infamy of Hermione.

MEASURE FOR MEASURE.
Act V. Scene 1. *page* 402.

Duke.   laws for all faults
But faults so countenanc'd, that the strong statutes
Stand like the *forfeits* in a barber's shop,
As much the mock as mark.

This is as curious a blunder as that in the preceding Play ; and as various have been the attempts to force its elucidation ; nay, forgery, it is said, was adopted by Mr. Kenrick to give a list of the supposed *forfeits* which Barber-Surgeons exacted from those who deviated from their established rules !

On the absurd idea that such a custom ever prevailed, either on the Continent, or in England, I shall be silent ; satisfied that the passage is grossly corrupt is sufficient for me ; and to correct and restore the orignal text, will, I trust be sufficient for my readers.

This error, like numbers of the same class, originates from mistake of sound : instead of *forceps,* the very sagacious transcriber gave the more familiar word—*forfeits.* The passage corrected affords a new figure.

                              laws for all faults ;
But faults so countenanc'd, that the strong statutes
Stand like the *forceps* in a barber's shop,
As much the mock as mark.

The exasperated Duke considers his laws as *mocked* by the people, and that they afford as much food for merriment, as loungers in a *barber's shop* derive, by playing tricks on each other with the *forceps* which is exposed as a *mark* of his profession. Thus the *forceps in a barber-surgeon's shop*, became the *mock* of idlers, though exhibited as a *mark* of surgical knowledge; and in like manner, the Duke's laws had become the *mock* of the dissolute, though they were the *mark* of legislative wisdom.

TROILUS AND CRESSIDA.

Act I. Scene 3. *page 263.*

ULYSSES.   And such again
As venerable Nestor *hatch'd* in silver.

The compositor, from the word not being sufficiently distinct in the copy, *hatch'd* and brought forth an egregious blunder; and which blunder has brought forth three pages of learned notes. It is unnecessary to adduce argument to show the imbecility of the word *hatch'd;* the passage when corrected, will prove Shakspeare's unerring genius.

And such again,
As venerable Nestor *harp'd* in silver,
Should with a bond, &c.

His eloquence, sweetly soft and harmoniously grand, operated on the sense of his auditors as music produced by the fingers of experience from a *harp* strung with *silver strings.*

In the subsequent speech the musical voice of Nestor is again complimented,

" We shall hear musick, wit, and oracle."

In defence of Dr. Johnson's opinion of this passage, I reluctantly refer the reader to Mr. Malone's note.

ULYSSES.   Should with a bond of *air* (strong as the axle-tree
On which Heaven rides,) knit all the Greekish ears
To his experienced tongue.

A bond of air! This I profess beyond my comprehension: and how *air* is to become a solid body, and form a *bond, strong as the axle-tree on which Heaven rides,* is, I believe, beyond human comprehension. Our author is styled, and justly too, the Poet of Nature; but, if this be natural, then has nature, in this instance, exposed a figure to her favorite as heterogeneous to physics as is the idea of—seeing a sound! And yet, Mr. Malone, in his note on this passage, observes, " With respect to the breath or speech of Nestor, here called *a bond of air*, it is so truly *Shaksperian*, that I have not the smallest doubt of the genuineness of the expression." Well, let us see if we can defend our author again.

In many parts of our author's plays, he has displayed a partiality for forensic terms, (French, perhaps, more particularly.) We must admit that the *axle-tree* of a carriage is either of *forged* or *cast steel*. The French word for *steel* is *acier ;* in old French, *acyre*. Formerly the word *air* was spelt *ayre*. Now look to the similarity of the letters which compose *acyre* and *ayre :* there is a *c* in the one word which is not required in the other. Suppose then the word *acyre* to have been perfect in the manuscript, and with which word, the person who read to the transcriber was unacquainted,—Would he not, most probably, sound it *asayre ?* Consequently, the transcriber, equally ignorant of the word which the passage required, wrote—a bond of *as ayre :* and thus the proof sheet came to the corrector, who expunged the superfluous *as*, and left the *bond of air*, or *ayre*, for critical animadversion.

Now let us read the passage corrected, and I am bold enough to say, according to the author's original text :

> And such again,
> As venerable Nestor *harp'd* in silver,
> Should, with a bond of *acier* (strong as the axle-tree
> On which Heaven rides,) knit all the Greekish ears
> To his experienc'd tongue.

If elucidation be necessary, it is merely to inform the reader that *acier* is the French word for *steel*.

MERRY WIVES OF WINDSOR.

ACT I. SCENE 3. *page* 40.

FALSTAFF.   I spy entertainment in her ; she discourses, she *carves*, she gives the leer of invitation.

No doubt Mrs. Ford was an excellent *carver*, and entertained her friends with choice viands ; but the *entertainment* to which Falstaff alludes, being that of love, her adroitness in the art of *carving* is not absolutely necessary.

Falstaff has *spied* a certain *craving* in the eye of the Merry Wife ; and as she has already given him the *leer of invitation*, he, in his lascivious manner, says,—

———— she *craves*, she gives the leer of invitation.

See a subsequent speech in this scene where Falstaff says,—

" O, she did so course o'er my exteriors with such a *greedy intention*, that the *appetite of her eye* did seem to scorch me like a burning glass."

And by *the appetite of her eye*—Falstaff judges he knows that for which *she craves*, or has a longing. The transposing of one letter gives the original reading.

SHOULD the works of our Immortal Bard derive additional lustre from my labours, the ambition of being considered a Commentator will scarcely be attributed to me, when I declare, that chance alone led me into this kind of study.

It was early in the ninth year of my captivity, (being then a hostage* in France,) that a fellow prisoner favoured me with a few volumes of Johnson and Steevens' edition of Shakspeare: they were truly a treat! To the rich repast I sat down, and from day to day regaled myself with the text. Having read the plays with attention, I re-commenced their perusal; resorting at each reference to the notes, to see how far my comprehension of the Poet corresponded with the illustrations of our highly learned Commentators; as also, to seek instruction from their observations. Here the variety of opinions awakened me first to reflection. I had met with many misconstructions; and, from my practical knowledge of the Typographic art, perceived, in many instances, that the Commentators had totally perverted the author's sense, by changing words, in each of which, the transposition of a single letter was only required to restore the original reading. However, still the idea of taking up my pen on the occasion was distant from my thoughts: but when I began to *compare notes* on that passage in Antony and Cleopatra, where seven pages displayed a controversy, in which every opinion was palpably erroneous, I judged, that whatever aid I could give towards restoring the original readings, and in illustrating the works of a Poet, whose fame must exist whilst British literature retains a name in polished Europe, would be favourably received; and in this I was the more confident, from the elevated terms in which the Commentators testified their approbation, where any happy correction or elucidation occurred. With marked attention I now compared each note with the text, many of which were truly judicious, interesting, and highly entertaining; but many others, with all due deference to the great characters who wrote them, I found to possess laboured investigation without utility; forced meaning without a rational foundation; great learning without elucidation; and approbation so marked, that the criterion for all future ages seemed unchangably determined: nor was the text supposed liable to farther correction, for one of Shakspeare's best Commentators observes,—" *The text is now established:*" but how far he was correct in this assertion, let even these Examples of *Seven Hundred Errors* evince.

And here it may be permitted me to say, that no person ever sat down to comment on the works of Shakspeare under so many disadvantages and inconveniencies: I had not a single volume from which I could derive the slightest assistance, save, that occasionally, I borrowed a pocket dictionary: the errors were conspicuous, the corrections false, and the author misinterpreted; to discriminate these led to correction; and in illustrating our author I soon perceived that common sense was the most certain guide. But miserably was I situated for study! Daily I awakened to the torments of lawless bondage! Lawless, because not originating from the ordinary chances of war:— a Tyrant's mandate forged my fetters!— I became as the bond of my Sovereign, on which execution would be levied, if reprisal were demanded:—Fate signed the deed:— it was witnessed by Misfortune; and redeemable only,— by Political Covenant! To these, and they cannot be called minor obstructions to study, I had to endure the constant noise of the saw and mallet which came from a carpenter's work-shop; whilst, beneath my chamber, five or six sons of Crispin were alternately at their hammer and lap-stone; but more tormenting than all, in a back house, opposite my window, were some chanting mantua-makers, whose discordant notes would have made Amphion break his lyre and forswear harmony!—I was more tormented than Hogarth's enraged musician, or an orator upon the hustings encountering the hisses of an enraged populace! But reading and writing proved the only balms to lull distraction; and while thus employed I forgot captivity, and that indigence had supplanted opulence at my table. Thus amused, besides some trifling productions which I published in Verdun, I wrote eight Dramatic pieces; and found, that even in captivity, consolation is not denied to persevering equanimity. But of what utility is my perseverance? my early prospects in life have been all blasted by captivity; and since I have been restored to liberty, I have sought patronage,—but in vain. This is an effort which becomes more public, and pride submits to an avowal, that unpatronised, the Immortal Bard, whose unerring genius I defend, must still remain exposed to illiberal and unjust reprehension.

Proposals

For Publishing by Subscription, *Seven Hundred Errors Corrected and Illustrated in* SHAKSPEARE's PLAYS; and of which this Pamphlet contains several Examples.

I. NOTWITHSTANDING the Author of the *Pursuits of Literature* exclaims against Printing on *wove paper*, this Work shall be printed with a perfectly *new type*, and on the best *wove paper*.

II. It shall consist of Four Parts; each part to contain One Hundred and Twenty pages; which will be bound in a similar manner to the Quarterly Reviews—the price of each *Part* to Subscribers, Three Shillings and Sixpence. To Non-Subscribers, Four Shillings.

III. As soon as the Author is honoured with a sufficient Number of Subscribers to defray the Expences attached to Printing, the work will be put to Press; and which period he most respectfully hopes the admirers of the *Great British Bard* will not suffer to be far distant.—He anticipates being able to publish the First Part early in November; and a succeeding Part every Fortnight after the delivery of the First, until finished.

IV. As the Author's circumstances, after enduring *Eleven Years Captivity in France*, compel him to adopt this mode of Publication, he most respectfully, would hope for payment on the delivery of each Part; that thereby he may be the better enabled to facilitate the Printing of the residue of the Work.

V. The Subscribers' Names to be published as encouragers of the Work.

John Hill, Printer, 52, Water Lane, Blackfriars.

Lightning Source UK Ltd.
Milton Keynes UK
UKOW07f1839160717
305433UK00004B/79/P